History of Taiwan

A Captivating Guide to Taiwanese History and the Relationship with the People's Republic of China

Free Bonus from Captivating History (Available for a Limited time)

Hi History Lovers!

Now you have a chance to join our exclusive history list so you can get your first history ebook for free as well as discounts and a potential to get more history books for free! Simply visit the link below to join.

Captivatinghistory.com/ebook

Also, make sure to follow us on Facebook, Twitter and Youtube by searching for Captivating History.

Contents

Introduction

The history of Taiwan is astonishing. The societies of the Neolithic Era in around 3000 BCE seemed to have been determined by the topology of the island. The original ethnic identity of the indigenous peoples is most likely Austronesian, that is, from the Philippines, Oceania (South Pacific), Malaya, and Madagascar. Some of the Chinese from the Sui dynasty between the years of 581 and 618 came along later. This mixture of people settled on the lower highlands of the Central Mountain Range, the principal mountain range of Taiwan. There they farmed on terraces and hunted long-horned deer on the slopes. Along the western and southern coasts, the people fished. Oysters, in particular, are still extremely common, and it isn't unusual to find empty shells along the shore from the feasts of rodents and weasels. Some of the basin area was so wet that the bamboo houses were built on stilts. Today, oyster omelets are popular, and every tourist should sample them.

Politically, Taiwan— was a warlord culture. The Portuguese, when passing by the island in the mid-1540s, called the island "Ilha Formosa," which means "Beautiful Island." Then the Dutch came in the 1620s, searching for a base of operations for the Dutch East India Company. Relations between these strangely garbed, foreign-speaking white men and the people of this sub-tropic island were puzzling and difficult.

Then the Han Chinese came in the 17th century. Many of these Han Chinese were refugees from the wars in China. This influx caused an explosive reaction. For years, the relationships between the peoples on the island vacillated from beneficial to hostile, as it was a clash of civilizations. Many of the Dutch trading colonies eventually became lucrative for both native and immigrant populations, who did intermingle and intermarry. Chinese junks, an ancient Chinese sailing ship that is still used today, sailed the waters, along with the expected pirates that raided the shores and seas carrying opium to China and Taiwan.

The Taiwanese threw out their sea-serpent mythical gods in favor of the time-honored beliefs of Taoism and Confucianism, which many envious Westerners struggle to learn even today.

And then came the Japanese in 1894! Taiwan was subjugated to a Japanese program of inculcation. All the people of Taiwan had to learn Japanese, and Shinto shrines cropped up everywhere. The Japanese overlords were at times tyrannical, and the Chinese and Taiwanese people who lived there created stronger bonds with each other. That's when the rebellions started, and they continued for years until they merged into the period of the two World Wars.

Then came Chiang Kai-shek in 1949. He awakened the conflict between the vestiges of Japanese influences and the Republic of China. In fact, many of the Japanese who were living in Taiwan were repatriated.

Having been inflicted with so many cultural and political invasions, a new breed of Taiwanese people rose up, and they wanted freedom from the oppression they had faced for decades, although there were some who wanted socialism and communism. Taiwan is not even recognized as an independent sovereign by every country in the world today. Read Taiwan's story—a story of an island that walks a tightrope searching for its identity, balance, and fate.

Chapter 1 – Formosa: Beautiful Island

Around 3000 BCE, it is thought that people came to Taiwan from the islands and countries in Southeast Asia, such as Malaysia, Madagascar, and Polynesia. In those days, a land bridge was there, so flora and fauna likewise migrated over to Taiwan with them. Due to the existence of that land bridge, Taiwan wasn't an island. That didn't happen until the seas rose, engulfing the land bridge and turning it into what is now the Taiwan Strait. Yu Shan, or Mount Yu, looms over the northeastern area of the island at almost 13,000 feet. To the west of the Taiwanese mountain chain are the lowlands.

The Taiwanese were hardy tribes of indigenous peoples, which included the Siraya, a community that is still around today, who came to grow rice, sugar cane, and foxtail millet on terraces hewn into the highlands and raise their cattle on the lower slopes. There were also Plains Aborigines, or Makatao, who settled in the lowlands. The Taivoan people settled in the hills and basin area, and the Paiwan people lived in the southcentral mountainous area. The farms of these peoples were designed in concentric rings. The inner ring was for their homes and gardens, the secondary ring for a family's plantings, and the third ring for the family vegetables. The rest of the agricultural land was for the entire community. Their homes of bamboo and thatch were built on stilts, and the people made offerings to gods like *Shou*, also known as the god of longevity. He was the god to whom the people appealed to in order to keep the waters from rising too high and drowning out their homes and lands.

The women tilled the fields on the higher plateaus, and the men hunted for *gtsod*, a horned Tibetan antelope, or they fished. The men of the lowlands hunted the sika deer and the sambar deer. There was a wealth of marine life just off the western shore with oysters being the most popular. Their calcite shells could be carved into cutting tools. The aborigines also fashioned clever saw-like knives called adzes, made from stone and later on flint. The people drank rice wine, and the women made rice balls for their husbands to take with them on the hunt.

The Siraya is a matriarchal society, and women once served as priestesses and oracles. A woman's future husband married into her family, but this only happened after he was thirty years old when he no longer hunted. The aboriginal men from both the plains and the highlands were expected to be prepared militarily.

The Headhunters!

Except for the Yami people, a group who still lives on Orchid Island in the Taiwan Strait, and the Ivantan people, the aboriginal people of Taiwan practiced headhunting. The Yami people is simply another name for the Tao people. Their god was Simo-Rapao, and headhunting was a breach of the Tao belief in him as Simo-Rapao considered all life to be sacred.

The raids mostly originated from the people in the highlands. Once they slew their victims from the lowland tribes, they removed the victims' heads. It was a gruesome process. The skin would be removed first by making an incision behind the ear. Once it was separated from the skull, a small wooden ball would be inserted in order to maintain its shape after shrinking. The lips were sewn shut, and the flesh was boiled in water containing tannins. Tannins are

4

plant-based mixtures or sap from oak bark that acts as an astringent, thus shrinking the skin around the ball. They then covered the skin with ash in order to keep the vengeful soul, called the *Muisak*, from escaping. Warriors carried the shrunken heads around as trophies, but they only did so temporarily as they were needed for future religious ceremonies.

It was believed that headhunting reduced the power of an enemy tribe. What's more, it was felt that the person who had been killed would serve his killer for the remainder of his days.

Coming and Going of the Chinese

An ancient historian, Ma Tuan-hiu, related that the Chinese people from the mainland raided Taiwan in the 7th century BCE. They landed on the southern coast, demanding tribute from the people in the lowlands for their leaders in the Chinese Sui dynasty. Stubbornly, the Siraya refused. The marauders burned their bamboo villages, and many were mercilessly slaughtered. Then their blood was used to make caulking for their boats, horrifying the survivors. But still, the survivors refused to pay the tribute. Some fled to the hills and mountains, but others stood their ground. Frustrated by these "wild men of the South," as they called them, the Chinese left without the demanded tribute.

Tahu Iron

The Taiwanese aborigines noticed the iron weapons and body decorations of the Chinese. The Tahu Culture, descendants from the aborigines of southern Taiwan, also wanted to learn the skill. Not only was it useful for themselves, but it could also be traded with other visiting peoples. From the year 400 BCE, they mined it in the mountainous regions, but the extraction process wasn't easy. The people built what were called "bloomeries," or clay furnaces. On the base, they placed charcoal and the ore, originally in the form of stone flecked with reddish streaks. The impurities were oxidized and left the oven through a small chimney. What was left after the other elements were mostly burned away was a crude form of iron. When it is hot, it is spongy, so the early blacksmiths were able to hammer it into their desired shapes. From the Tahu people, the practice spread to the Niaosung Culture, among others. Iron was also used for primitive coinage.

Chapter 2 – The Arrival of the Chinese and Their Religion

There was an influx of people from China into Taiwan starting in the 3rd century CE. During those early centuries, there were three main Chinese kingdoms competing for power on the mainland—the Cao Wei, the Shu Han, and the Sun Wu. The Shu Han people primarily based their livelihoods on agriculture, and many were fishermen. Their state was saturated by the Yellow River, a mighty river that brought bounty, but with it also came floods and drought when the river dried up. In those primitive days, the people of that age told their histories through myths and legends. They once told the tale of a great drought in the story of their mythical hero, the giant Kua Fu. He was kind and wanted to help his people who were starving in the sweltering heat while their plants died. He looked angrily upon the sun and felt that he should teach it a lesson. He decided he was going to chase and capture the great sun in the east. Hastily, he ran, but he stopped often to drink of the waters from the streams and rivers, including the Wei River. He kept running and running but became so very thirsty that he drank the Yellow River dry. Exhausted after days of running, he collapsed and died. From where his body lay, a great grove of peaches grew, thus feeding and quenching the thirst of the people.

In the 3rd century, the Three Kingdoms warred with each other. The Cao Wei settled in the north (where the Wei River of the myth is located) and then moved into what is now northern China. The Cao Wei then conquered the land of the Shu Han, where peaches were grown in abundance (it is also the location of the Donglin Forest). The Sun Wu (or Dong Wu) people settled around the Yangtze River in the eastern region. They were traders, and the people also mined crude metals and dried seawater for salt.

In 222, the Sun Wu managed to free themselves from the rule of the Cao Wei and became its own empire seven years later. A year later, in 230, the Sun Wu touched upon the shores of Taiwan.

Confucianism

The people of Taiwan sought to move beyond the myth and magic that permeated their culture, and they looked toward the Han people, a collective term that refers to the Chinese, and one of their religions, Confucianism, to help do so. As they were mostly tillers of the earth and seas, they saw their lives as cycles. For every day, there was a night, and the seasons fell into a pattern. Confucius was a religious scholar who looked upon the whole of the earth and heaven as a never-ending cycle of the yin and the yang, ever circling but spiraling toward unity. He also taught compassion as it brought peace. Too many bloody wars were fought that conflicted with the happiness that everyone deserved. It was the objective of all humanity to achieve unity, a oneness, with life. He spoke not of a personal god but the essence of love and of life.

Tian, in Confucianism, is the god of heaven to whom one owes respect and the performance of sacred rituals to demonstrate that belief. Tian is eternal and judges all the people, regardless of whether they are good or evil. According to the Confucian philosopher Xunzi, "Tian's course has regularities, which don't exist for the sage, Yao, and then disappear for the tyrant, Jie."

The five principles of this tradition are *Ren* (humaneness), *Yi* (righteousness), *Li* (rite), *Zhi* (knowledge), and *Xin* (integrity). Confucius eschewed the barbarity of the headhunters of the past and the greediness of those who led only by virtue of birth, responding with an alternative way to live. He called that way the "middle path." It is the road that leads between heaven and earth. It sprouts from the *li*, which is the interaction of all that lies between humans, objects, and states, such as laughing and mourning. A true understanding of the principles of *li* will lead to balance. Confucius valued loyalty to one's ruler but would recommend rebellion if that ruler was deemed truly evil—a little known fact of this teaching.

Ancestor worship is a misnomer often applied to the Chinese. It is not "worship" per se; it is more of a reverence for one's ancestors. Even today, Chinese Christians will have annual ceremonies respecting the memories of their ancestors. They still carve figures of their immediate ancestors out of soapstone or jade, and one can see stone figures of elderly men with canes, fishermen, women carrying leaves, and teachers with scrolls. It is still believed today that one's ancestors still protect and guide them. Soapstone is a metamorphic rock with a high talc content and is one of the softest of stones. Jade is a more expensive stone composed of aluminum and calcite. It has a green tint, which is the color of vitality and life.

Taoism

The Han people brought Taoism with them when they moved to Taiwan, which is a belief in the immortality of the human soul, but it is an immortality that can only be achieved by observing the precepts of the Tao, which literally translated means "the way."

The Tao is a belief in the universe and the oneness of life. It requires austerity and the practice of a virtuous life. Like Confucianism, it is about a balance as one is expected to live a life in harmony with the natural world. Taoism implies an afterlife exists but never focuses upon it as the Abrahamic religions do. Instead, it relates to a transformation from the corporal self to the enlightened spirit, what some refer to as the "soul."

The roots of Taoism go back to the 4th and 3rd centuries BCE, but its most famous spokesman was Lao Tzu. He exalted the idealistic leader as one who "is best when people barely know he exists. When his work is done, his aim fulfilled, people will say they did it themselves."

Taoism values simplicity and sees life as a process created by the yin and yang. The earth is viewed as a creative, dynamic progression. Taoists are pantheistic and believe in many deities. The highest deity is Yu Huang, who is never-changing and rules with compassion and understanding. Symbolically, he is represented by the sun, the moon, and the progeny of their union. Yu Huang is the god of the living and the dead, and he passes judgment on deceased souls and pronounces their eternal fates.

Yellow Turban Rebellion

Zhang Jue, the leader of the Yellow Turban Rebellion, wrote about it, saying, "The Azure Sky is already dead; the Yellow Sky will soon rise." The "azure sky" refers to the Han government, and the "yellow sky" was the term Zhang Jue gave to the peasants who were laboriously working along the Yellow River and were being crushed by their emperor, Emperor Ling. Between the years 184 to 205 CE, the early followers of Taoism under Zhang Jue rebelled on behalf of the rough and labor-hardened peasants. They wore yellow turbans or scarves. The Han government might have prevailed, but the fields went fallow during the war, and famine followed. Those who could emigrated to Taiwan.

This 3rd-century rebellion harkened back to the peaceful period of the Yellow Emperor, that is, Huangdi from the ancient period. Some believe he was a prominent leader who was later deified, while others believe he was a god that became incorporated into the list of historical figures. Huangdi was a cosmic ruler who brought peace and prosperity, and he was the legendary hero of the people suppressed by the succession of imperialist and autocratic dynastic leaders.

Buddhism

Buddhism was brought to Taiwan during the Ming dynasty in the 17th century when the Dutch ruled the island. The people came from southeastern China but had to keep their practices hidden, as the Dutch had mistaken their statues of Wusheng Laomu, the ancient mother goddess, and Guanyin, the goddess of compassion, not as the representations of the spiritual figures they represent but as the gods (idols) themselves.

The object of this religion is enlightenment, that is, a state of ultimate peace within the self and the union of the self with the world without its disruptive emotions and negativities. From this freedom flows wisdom. The noble truths that exist are existence in suffering (dukkha), the case of suffering which is earthly desire (trishna), the cessation of suffering (nirvana), and the path of righteousness that springs from those principles.

Buddhism grew after the Dutch were ejected, and it is now the largest religion in Taiwan.

Chapter 3 – The Dutch Trading Years

Trade via the Junks

Located in the Taiwan Strait are the Penghu Islands, a collection of islands which were settled by the Han people. Many of the early Taiwanese people established fishing villages there. They sailed the Taiwan Strait and the western Pacific in classic Chinese junks. The junk is a vessel built of wood with a bamboo interior. For a sealant, lime was mixed with tung oil, which was obtained from the tung tree. Tung oil has the characteristic of hardening almost upon contact. Later on, *ch-nam* was the tree resin used for caulking. Inside the junk, there was a multitude of inner compartments which served to hold off flooding. The American inventor, Benjamin Franklin, used chambers designed after the Chinese junks to keep the mail dry when he was shipping packets of it across the Atlantic.

Most junks have a centerboard which protrudes from the keel and helps stabilize the vessel. The maritime fishermen of the Penghu Islands and southern Taiwan created retractable centerboards because some of the waters were shallow. Later colonists who visited Taiwan adopted them.

After iron was discovered in Taiwan, iron tools, raw iron, silver, and white or blue/white porcelain pots and drinking vessels were shipped in mercantile junks. The products were shipped along a route called the Maritime Silk Road that connected China, Southeast Asia, India, the Arabian Peninsula, Somalia, Egypt, and Europe. In exchange, the junks carried spices such as pepper, frankincense, and dragon's blood, which was a reddish-colored resin used for varnish and even medicine, back to Taiwan.

Pottery

Archeologists found many beautiful pots and water and wine vessels made of clay dating back to the 9th and 10th centuries BCE in Taiwan. The background is light-colored, and linear and spherical designs appear darker when the clay is dried. The darker lines (or "red cords") are created by halting the firing process and covering the linear and spherical areas with ropes before reheating the pottery. Another technique they used was the impressment of coiled basket-weave over the vessel.

Chinese pottery was also manufactured in the kilns of Taiwan. The people had learned new techniques of heating their kilns up to 1400° Celsius (over 2550° Fahrenheit). That transformed the clay/quartz mixture and gave the pottery a translucent quality.

The Dutch vs. the Chinese and the Aborigines

In the early 1600s, Taiwan was mostly visited by Chinese fishermen, pirates, and smugglers. There were no permanent Chinese settlements other than those along the coasts. However, throughout the 1600s, maritime Spanish, Japanese, Chinese, English, and Dutch traders all wanted to convert Taiwan into peaceful trading colonies where herbs and metals could be produced and sold by the trading companies.

The Dutch East India Company was the first to try to do so, attempting to establish a post on the Penghu Islands in 1622, but they were driven off by Ming forces. Their ships, under the command of Marten Sonck, were forced to abandon the area after the brutal attacks of the Chinese and island warriors under Generals Yu and Wang Megxiong.

From there, the Dutch moved south and invaded a peninsula in the Anping District where they set up a huge fort called Fort Zeelandia in 1624. The Dutch and the original aborigine tribesmen were determined to pacify the hostile Chinese in order to establish a trading colony from which they could ship herbs, spices, iron, silver, and gold. In particular, Mattau, now the modern-day Madou District, in the lower hills and basin area of Taiwan where the Taivoan aborigines live, resisted the Dutch influx with great ferocity, killing Dutch soldiers and destroying their buildings. The Dutch sent in reinforcements and were finally able to subdue the people who lived there in 1635.

After successive attacks, the Dutch were able to control a number of villages, including Sakam, Soulang, Bakloan, and Sinkan. The people at the villages engaged in local trade with each other, providing their neighbors with venison, fish, and firewood, but they disliked interference. Eventually, the indigenous peoples established a working relationship with the Dutch, but it was short-lived. The tribes sometimes raided each other, started insurrections, and still went on head-hunting expeditions. To make matters worse, Chinese and Japanese pirates raided the towns from offshore.

In addition to the pirate raids, war erupted between the Chinese from the Ming Dynasty and the Dutch at sea. In 1633, the Chinese admiral Zheng Zhilong defeated the Dutch at the Battle of Liaoluo Bay. The inner revolts and rebellions continued until many of the people of Taiwan saw that those who had established relations with the Dutch were at peace. More and more villages came forward and offered peace in exchange for Dutch protection. That peace, known as the *pax Hollandica*, happened in 1636, and it showed that the Dutch

East India Company now had firm control of the southwest of the island, which they referred to as Formosa. After that, the Dutch leased their owned land to the native farmers and fishermen and taxed them as well.

The Dutch also promoted the migration of Chinese Han immigrants. However, the relationship between the two failed when Dutch officials raised taxes and were found to be corrupt, as some demanded sexual favors from aboriginal women as well as gifts of pelts and rice. As a result, an uprising occurred in 1652 called the Guo Huaiyi Rebellion. The Dutch put down the rebellion, killing 25 percent of those that participated and selling others into slavery. They also placed a ban on their provisions of iron and salt.

Fall of Fort Zeelandia and Dutch Colonies

Fort Zeelandia sat at one entrance to the U-shaped Liaoluo Bay, while a sister fort, Fort Provintia, was at the other end. In 1661, a Chinese leader by the name of Zheng Chenggong, better known as Koxinga, a Ming loyalist and warrior, wanted to establish his own kingdom in the highly prized Dutch Zeelandia area. He sailed from the sea south of Taiwan and attacked Dutch musketeers, defeating them. The Dutch then attacked the Chinese junks, but Koxinga prevailed along the shore and built fortifications right near the fort. Later, his many warriors, equipped with body-length shields of iron, plowed right through the Dutch defenders and utterly massacred them. The remaining Dutch soldiers were still holed up in the garrison at Fort Zeelandia while the Chinese attackers engaged in massive attacks against their vanguard forces.

Seeing that the Chinese were about to prevail, the Taiwanese people from Sakam, Soulang, Bakloan, Sinkan, and other Dutch colonies allied themselves with the Chinese, putting the Dutch in a precarious position.

Koxinga was also allied with escaped slaves who knew how to use muskets, rifles, and cannons. Other Chinese sent out volleys of arrows against the Dutch. The Dutch had seriously misjudged the strength and ferocity of their foes and were slowly shoved toward the sea. According to the historian William Campbell, Koxinga's men "continually pressed onwards, notwithstanding many were shot down; not stopping to consider, but ever rushing forward like mad dogs."

Retaliatory Strikes and Torture

Once the word of this humiliating defeat reached the Dutch in their headquarters in Jakarta (on the current-day island of Java), they sent out more warships. Koxinga's men had blockaded Fort Zeelandia, so only small-scale operations were attempted at sea, but they all failed. A month later, another assault was initiated, but it was also repelled. The Dutch soldiers bravely held onto the garrison, but since they were running low on ammunition and supplies, they fled in 1662.

Koxinga essentially then assumed leadership of most of the aboriginal and Taiwanese settlers. Two months later, an offensive assault was again staged by Koxinga to rid Formosa of the rest of the Dutch. General Frederick Coyett of Fort Zeelandia and General Valentyn of Fort Provintia were forced to surrender against the might of the great Koxinga. Koxinga then renamed Formosa the Kingdom of Tungtu in 1662. The name was later changed to Tungning by his son.

Chapter 4 – The Ming, The Qing, and Japan: The War Years

Koxinga died only a few months after the fall of Fort Zeelandia, and his son, Zheng Jing, took over. He promoted Chinese migration in order to recruit those migrants into military service. He also wanted to prevent a takeover by the Qing dynasty of China, which was established in 1636. Zheng Jing granted free ownership of land to the peasants who worked the land and performed military service. Education all but halted.

In 1683, the remaining Ming loyalists who had settled in Taiwan couldn't hold out against the huge forces of the Qing dynasty, and Koxinga's grandson, Zheng Keshuang, was forced to surrender to the Qing dynasty.

The Dark Period

Xuanye, the fourth emperor of the Qing dynasty and also known as the Kangxi Emperor, had little interest in Taiwan. He called it a "ball of mud." Therefore, he restricted migration from mainland China and erected earthen fortresses between the plains to the west and the highlands in the east. Those with aboriginal routes tended to settle in the highlands when the Qing dynasty was unsuccessful in converting them into taxpayers. Those who lived in the west paid taxes to the Qing imperial magistrates and leased their land, mostly for farming.

The Qing also discovered that Taiwan was difficult to govern, as the ethnic clashes continued among Han and Hakka people, as well as with the remaining aboriginal peoples and alienated peoples from other cultures like the Japanese. Even Han clans from the smaller districts warred with each other.

Despite the limit on emigration from China, disaffected Chinese gradually relocated to Taiwan. By the early 19th century, there were two million Chinese immigrants.

The Opium Wars

Great Britain saw the strategic advantage of using China and Taiwan as trading centers. They coveted Taiwan most of all as it was entirely surrounded by water and therefore accessible to shipping. However, Taiwan and China did not see the value in British goods and refused to trade. So, in order to get their foot in the door, the British smuggled in opium from India as a way to control and corrupt the government and its policies. Once China realized what the British were doing, they attempted to put a stop to it. In 1839, Chinese officials demanded the British hand over opium stored in a warehouse. Tensions rose to the boiling point, and the First Opium War was started, which took place between the years 1839 and 1842.

The Chinese imperial troops and the British sailors competed with each other in terms of trade rather than cooperating, and hostilities broke out between them. The Chinese then set up a blockade against foreign vessels in the harbor of Hong Kong, which permitted Chinese monopolies, like the Cohong from the Canton province, to control the import-export business. The British retaliated by bombing the port of Tingha along with some other ports. The Qing warriors proved that they were not up to conducting battle against the guns and cannons of the British warships and finally surrendered in 1842. Now, the British were in control of Hong Kong trade.

As a result of the Treaty of Nanking (or Nanjing) of 1842, the Chinese agreed to pay an indemnity to Hong Kong and ceded it to the British. After successive negotiations, other ports were designated for the use of British-Chinese trade.

The Second Opium War was fought between China and the forces of Great Britain, France, and Russia between 1856 and 1860. The issues stemmed over the legalization of opium, an eradication of Chinese piracy, the regulation of the coolie system, and more open trade relations. The coolie system was the importation of Chinese workers who were basically treated as slaves. They were paid less than the native population but were promised health benefits in return. Although that might sound somewhat promising, those involved in the coolie system were often lied to in order to get them to sign a contract. They would at times be sold to work on projects far from their homeland, such as the United States, and many of them died under terrible, back-breaking conditions.

So, in 1856, the Western countries attacked and occupied the Canton Province. The governor of Canton surrendered, and the British and French gained control of many of the Chinese forts and burned the summer palace of Prince Gong, an imperial Manchu prince and an important statesman in the Manchu-led Qing dynasty, in Beijing. The Qing dynasty lost the war, and as a result, many more ports were open to European countries, opium was legalized, compensation was paid by the Chinese for piracy, and the coolie system was systematized.

Due to this war, there was a migration from Manchuria into mainland China and Taiwan. The people from Manchuria are called the Manchu people, and they are an ethnic minority. This migration continued into the 1940s, and even though they represented a minority, the Manchu people changed the cultural character and identity of Taiwan as time went on.

The Sino-French War in Taiwan

Much of the focus of the Sino-French War was directed toward Vietnam, just south of China in the delta regions. The territory of Tonkin and Annam were French protectorates, and the Chinese attempted to gain control of those areas, as it was a lucrative region for fishing and agriculture. The Chinese also wanted the presence of European colonies eliminated from the peninsula. In addition, the Chinese coastal provinces were charging enormous taxes for the rights to trade, and it was a source of great wealth.

The French also wanted the northern ports in Taiwan and targeted Keelung and Tamsui in 1884. There were also rich iron mines in that area, some run by the British colonists. The British, who were already established in some of the towns, didn't want to become involved in this new war. The Qing dynasty heroically defended the area, putting most of his emphasis on Tamsui. It had the support of the Han people from the hills, who set up torpedoes and land mines and used long-range rifles called matchlocks. The Han were skilled marksmen, and they had been hardened by war. The Han incurred many severe wounds and mutilations during the battles, but the hospital there was excellent, so many of them left to fight another day.

At Tamsui, the French built a new fort, Fort Neuf, to protect the entrance to the Tamsui River. The French frigates moved into the area where they disembarked and moved inland to confront the Chinese defenders. The battlefield was full of natural obstacles— spiny plants, tall hedges, scrub brush, and deep ditches. Within that territory, the Chinese warriors hid. A huge firefight broke out in October 1884, filling the air with dust and gunpowder. The French companies became separated and were shoved back by the mighty troops of Sun Kaihua. The French fired and fired, sometimes just into the empty air, and since their bugler had been shot, they couldn't sound for a ceasefire. Thus, the troops continued to shoot until they were precariously low on ammunition. Finally, they heard a frantic call for retreat, and they raced toward the shore to board their waiting boats in the rough waters. Some of the French ships capsized in the process. The head of the forces, Captain Garnot, later said, "The courage and dash shown by our officers and sailors, who had not been trained for a land battle, cannot conceal the fact that we opened fire in a disorderly manner...that our troops lost our heads, firing wildly at the enemy and using their ammunition in a few minutes."

One of their most influential naval admirals, Amédée Courbet, called the French action in Taiwan "irrelevant." In view of the fact that France considered Tonkin in North Vietnam to be more valuable, they evacuated northern Taiwan and the Pescadores Islands just offshore. A preliminary accord between China and France was drawn up in 1884, followed by the Treaty of Tientsin in 1885. As a result of the treaty, France surrendered its interest in Taiwan and was allowed to retain their protectorate in Vietnam.

Gruesome Executions

In the Tamsui marketplace, the heads of the French fighters were displayed on pikes, along with body parts, including legs, arms, and hands. These barbaric practices were mostly inflicted by the hands of the Hakka warriors, that is, the native people from the hills. The Chinese general, Sun Kaihua, however, had them buried reverently where they fell. Sun Kaihua gave tribute to the goddess Mazu, and the emperor, Li Hung-Chang, said, "The goddess has been kind to people and kind to myself."

The Japanese Invasion of Taiwan

In 1894, Japan and China went to war. The Japanese craved many of the lands in northern China and attacked there, starting with Manchuria. The Japanese were quite successful against the poorly equipped Chinese troops there. Then their ambitions moved to the rich lands of southern China, wanting to gain these lands, which included Taiwan, in the peace treaty that would be signed to end the war. However, Taiwan and the Penghu Islands were excluded from the armistice. So, the Japanese attacked the Penghu Islands, managing to take it over in a matter of days. Once the main garrisons of the Penghu Islands were captured, there was little interest on the part of the Taiwanese to fight. Japan had control of much of China already and was quite strong. Prime Minister Hirobumi Itō and diplomat Mutsu Munemitsu of Japan negotiated with Li Hongzhang and Li Jingfang of the Qing dynasty, who was currently in control of Taiwan. Although the Qing representatives desperately tried to negotiate a truce, they didn't have the strength to prevail over the Japanese. Hence, they were forced to turn over all of Taiwan to Japan. In April 1895, Japan offered a treaty to Taiwan, the Treaty of Shimonoseki, which ceded control over Taiwan, and the government reluctantly signed it.

Uproar Over Taiwan

Qiu Fengjia, a Hakka patriot living in Taiwan, set up a brief republic in the country protected by a militia that he had spent his wealth on after the Qing dynasty had ceded its rights to Taiwan. However, an influx of nearly 10,000 Japanese soldiers descended upon the administration, terminating it and attacking the country, killing men, women, and children alike. They set fire to their homes and farms. The Taiwanese defenders fought a guerilla-style war and inflicted more damage upon the Japanese than would be expected. These Taiwanese were fiercely independent. Although the Japanese-appointed Governor-General, Kabayama Sukenori, reported to Tokyo that the "island is secured," it wasn't. Unrest fomented among the people. In the north, there were riots and rebellions monthly.

For inspiration, the local people told tales about Liao Tianding, a man who stole from the Japanese. Liao advocated continued uprising against Japanese rule, and legends about him cropped up everywhere in Taiwan. He was thought of as a "Robin Hood-like figure." Stories about healings that took place upon his intercession circulated. Others claimed to have seen his ghost and indicated he had saved the lives of ill people and reversed the fortunes of the poor. Shrines were built in his honor, and children's books were written with the theme of being courageous against oppression.

The short-lived Republic of Formosa lasted from May to October of 1895.

Chapter 5 – Japanese Taiwan

The "Gotō" Theory

Gotō Shinpei was a leading politician in Japan, and he was appointed as the head of the civilian affairs of Taiwan. Gotō believed in developing a theoretical structure that suited the personalities of the people, one that respected their histories and traditions and preserved their culture. He called this his "biological principles."

Gotō intensely disliked giving any conquered countries the appearance of a military state, wanting the people to feel that they were worthy of making contributions to society. His teachers and officials wore secular clothing, and the military police was replaced by a civilian-recruited police force. As heads of departments, he recruited the elder Taiwanese statesmen, as they knew the people well. There was a serious health problem on the island due to the rampant addiction to opium. Opium addiction was rampant in China and spread via the Han Chinese who settled in Taiwan. The government knew it would be impossible to eradicate opium entirely in the beginning, so they restricted its usage, and the authorities took over the opium trade. Albeit, that was a questionable solution because the government made a large profit on opium. Opium addiction was significantly reduced, though. There were anti-drug campaigns, and rehabilitation clinics opened, but opium wasn't outlawed until the mid-1940s. Gotō's ultimate objective was the total elimination of opium and with it the disintegration of all the criminal enterprises that sold the drug.

Industry

Gotō then laid the foundation for finance. Via the passage of the Bank Act of Taiwan in 1897, the island's first bank, the Bank of Taiwan, was founded in 1899. Gotō's purpose in doing that was to create a stable currency system in order to encourage investment by foreign countries as well as the citizens themselves. The bank also provided loans for people wishing to start new businesses. In the Bank of Taiwan, there was a national treasury, and its first currency was the Taiwanese yen. Unlike Western banks, the Bank of Taiwan was comprised of departments particularly fashioned to cater to various industries as well as those designated for government purposes. There were divisions for managing the finances for fields involved in precious metals, accounting, legal affairs, real estate, and even human resources.

Some of the largest corporations in the world found their histories intertwined with the Bank of Taiwan, which encouraged progress and development. Two of the largest are the Mitsubishi Corporation and the Mitsui Group.

China & Taiwan: World War I

In 1912, while Japan maintained colonial occupation of Taiwan, Chinese revolutionaries overthrew the last dynasty of China—the Qing dynasty. This development influenced the development of Taiwan in the years to come.

Sun Yat-sen was the vociferous leader of a new nationalist movement and established the Republic of China. This republic would have a president, with Sun Yat-sen being the first, and delegates from each of the provinces. A constitution was drawn up, as well as a bicameral legislature. Sun Yat-sen asked the provinces to set up a National Assembly, and he stepped down as president in 1912. The capital was then moved to Beijing. Two political parties were also on the rise—the Tongmenghui, the party led by Song Jiaoren, and the Republican Party, headed up by Yuan Shikai. The Tongmenghui reorganized and became the Kuomintang (also known as the Nationalist Party of China). However, the Republican Party did not last long, as it was only around for a little over a year.

During World War I (1914 to 1918), China and Japan provided supportive roles by keeping sea lanes open for the Allied Powers who were battling the Germans at sea. The Chinese didn't participate as soldiers but provided equipment maintenance, manned factories, and manufactured and shipped ammunition to the Allied countries. The war was won by the Allies, and Japan used that to gain some control in China. However, they were only able to get nominal control of the Shandong Province in northeastern China.

A happy result of World War I was the fact that it stimulated the economy of Taiwan. Their total farm production quadrupled, imports increased substantially, and so did its exports. The port of Keelung, built in 1896 in northeastern Taiwan, was updated and expanded to allow for increased marketing activities. Plans were then laid for the development of another port at Gaoxiong (Kaohsiung) in southern Taiwan. That, in particular, would help the Japanese colonial administration do business in Southeast Asia as well as with China.

With the additional money pouring in after World War I, education increased, the growth of a business class developed, and private enterprises rose, although every company was required to submit to oversight by the colonial authorities. Social reform took place as well.

The Japanese government made it a practice to incorporate the historical and religious beliefs of the people of Taiwan into its culture. Nevertheless, they gradually tried to fix the traditional Japanese social structure into the minds of the people. This brought about the "Dōka," meaning "integration," which lasted between 1915 and 1937. In this framework, a sense of equality was fostered.

The push and pull of various societal pressures gave rise to various idealistic political philosophies: 1) the colonial paradigm, under which the colonial authorities are seen as protectors who also dispensed justice; 2) the Taiwanese nationalists who saw Taiwan as a separate and distinct culture with its own set of laws and expectations; 3) the Chinese nationalists of Taiwan who saw themselves as a part of China; and 4) the group who wanted to be perceived as Japanese.

Gotō Shinpei then reorganized the economy of Taiwan by nationalizing agriculture, finance, and education. He also added a flood-control program. To accelerate growth that wouldn't depend upon subsidies from Japan, he encouraged shipping. He also introduced a railroad system, hospitals, roads, and infrastructure, which accelerated the country into the modern age. Gotō's nationalism efforts did run into problems due to popular uprisings starting with his nationalization of the railway system.

The Wuchang Uprising

This rebellion occurred when Japan was nationalizing the railway system. Originally, the railways were financed by private investors, including foreign investors, and some segments of the railroad were locally financed and run. However, the financial system that fueled this railway construction venture went bankrupt in 1911. That bankruptcy didn't affect all the portions of the system. Despite the fact that the bankruptcy didn't affect all areas of the railway system, the Japanese government came in and nationalized the system anyway under what was called the Railway Protection Movement. Financiers were furious, giving rise to this revolt in the Hubei Province in China. Revolutionaries took over the Viceroy's residence and assumed control of the city of Huguang and eventually the whole area. This helped to lead to the gradual decline of the Qing dynasty and the Xinhai Revolution which followed.

Xinhai Revolution

The history of China and Taiwan overlapped throughout the 20th century, although there were distinct differences. Also known as the Chinese Revolution, this rebellion, which started in 1911 and ended in 1912, shook up the area because it consisted of a series of smaller uprisings in various parts of Taiwan and mainland China. It resulted in the overthrow of the last Chinese imperial dynasty, the Qing. The government that took over called itself the Republic of China under Sun Yat-sen.

The Tapani Incident

There was, however, perennial friction between the aboriginal population, the well-settled immigrant population, and the Japanese overlords. In 1915, during World War I, the aboriginal people rebelled. They were members of the aboriginal tribe who had originally settled in the hills and basin areas of Taiwan. This rebellion, called the Tapani Incident, was one of the uprisings staged by the people of the island who had come to resent the sovereignty of non-native people from other countries. In particular, they were opposed to the nationalization of the sugar and forestry industries.

These people cross-bred their societal structure with religious beliefs. They believed that a new age was dawning in Taiwan. It was needed, they said, as there were so many criminals who preyed upon the weaker members of society, and the Taivoan people and the Han Taiwanese believed that included corrupt and greedy leaders. They felt that an apocalyptical event was on the horizon that would bring about a new Utopian age. Those who partook in this incident felt that violence was needed in order to trigger this new age of peace and harmony. It was like a religion, or perhaps it would be better described as a cult, but its significance evidenced what might be best described as a "clash of civilizations," and the Taivoan occurrence was, in a sense, an omen of the transformation of Taiwan.

The Communist Party

In 1921, there were three separate governments in China, along with two minor breakaway entities. The only way that Yat-sen could establish a "One-China" policy, which would later include Taiwan, would be to delineate an understanding between his Kuomintang Party with the ever-growing Communist Party of China, which had been consuming the smaller factions. In 1923, he signed the Sun-Joffe Manifesto, which created a cooperative relationship among the various factions. Lenin, the head of Russia and the seat of the Communist Party, praised him for this move.

Musha Incident

In 1930, the Japanese government in Taiwan confiscated farmlands and rice paddies from the indigenous aborigine population in Taiwan. Men were gradually seized as slaves, along with their land. The women were molested and children maltreated. Taking advantage of a public event, the Association of Aboriginal People rebelled and killed about 130 Japanese soldiers, but only two Han Taiwanese were killed because they were dressed in Japanese clothing.

Japan treated the indigenous people differently than the later settlers in Taiwan. They considered them to be barbarians and took land from the indigenous farmers over the course of time. This land, by law, was reserved for the aboriginals, but the Japanese had little respect for the property allocations. "I think the Japanese incurred the wrath of our ancestors because they neglected the fact that we, the aboriginal people, have rights over land inherited from our ancestors," said Siyac, the leader of the aboriginal members.

Little by little, illegal land sales to the Han Chinese made it extremely difficult for the indigenous farmers to support themselves and their families because there wasn't enough land left for their farms.

The Mukden Incident/ Manchuria Incident

Even though this didn't take place in Taiwan proper, this takeover, which primarily involved the capital city of Mukden of Manchuria, affected Taiwan. In 1931, Japan was primarily concerned about expanding its occupied territory for the purposes of wealth and to create space for its growing population. A weak bombing of the Japanese-owned railroad was staged by Japan, which wanted to implicate China for the "attack." That way, they could use it as an excuse to go to war with China. As a consequence of this engagement, Japan took over all of Manchuria. They then set up a puppet government.

The Taiwan Exposition

In 1935, the transformation of Taiwan was exhibited in New Taipei City, which was formerly known as Keelung. It marked all of the achievements and advancements made by Taiwan to the world. Even the Republic of China admired all of the amazing accomplishments of the Taiwanese.

Members of the Taiwanese government began wearing civilian clothing rather than military uniforms, and finally, in 1935, the Taiwanese nationalists scored the majority in an election. Taiwan also gained representation in Japan proper in its administrative structure called the Imperial Diet. However, the Imperial Diet ended in 1947, shortly after World War II.

Chapter 6 – The Sino-Japanese War & World War II

The Shanghai Massacre–The Chinese Civil War

The Sun-Joffe Manifesto, which was agreed upon in 1923, was hardly enough to unite China and Taiwan. After the death of Sun Yat-sen, Chiang Kai-shek, a very powerful military leader of the Kuomintang (KMT), rose to power. He did so through armed uprisings, most of which were against the local warlords. Chiang Kai-shek's group was called the National Revolutionary Army (NRA).

By 1927, Chiang Kai-shek controlled the Wuhan, Nanchang, and Guangdong provinces. During that year, the Communists conspired to assassinate Chiang Kai-shek, but he discovered the plot and resolved to rid the country of the Communist Party. There were armed revolts and chaos in the area of Shanghai, which was led by student and labor leaders under Zhou Enlai and Chen Duxiu. As retribution for the planned assassination and the rise of the Chinese Communist Party, Chiang Kai-shek activated his KMT forces, and they tore through Shanghai in April 1927, beheading and slaughtering members of the Communist Party there. Some of the Communists were officially executed, and others went missing. It is estimated that as many as 5,000 to 10,000 people were killed. Mao Zedong, who later became Chairman Mao, and his forces were defeated by Chiang Kai-shek. Mao then retreated to the countryside. In 1928, Chiang Kai-shek was considered to be the leader of the Republic of China.

The Marco Polo Bridge Incident and the Second Sino-Japanese War

Near Peking, China, the Marco Polo Bridge, or the Logou, is a great stone bridge built in 1189 and restored in 1698. On July 7, 1937, Japanese troops opened fire on the Chinese troops southwest of Beijing. The skirmish went on in fits and starts. These incidents triggered a declaration of war between Japan and China, also known as the Second Sino-Japanese War, which then slid into World War II in 1939. (The First Sino-Japanese War was fought between 1894 and 1895 over the control of Korea.)

After negotiations, an uneasy truce was signed. However, the terms weren't consistently observed, and subsequent battles broke out. This more violent conflict was called the Battle of Beiping-Tianjin, also known as the Battle of Beijing, and it started in July and ended in August 1937. The battle raged on from one area to another. The Chinese had traditional weaponry, but the Japanese brought in air and naval support, so it turned into a bloody massacre, with Japan winning the battle in Beijing. However, the anti-Japanese campaign continued. By 1939, the Japanese forces were scattered throughout mainland China and were becoming thin. The war reached a stalemate.

The Japanese had slowly been conquering the islands in the Southern Pacific along with sections of mainland China, starting with the conquest of Taiwan back in 1895. They had envisioned an expanded Japanese empire, so they continued their attacks in Asia and the islands in the Pacific. In 1941, the Japanese, who had already joined the fray in World War II on the side of Germany and Italy, attacked the base of Pearl Harbor, located in Hawaii. The United States then formally entered the war. By 1942, four major counties had allied with each other—the United States, the Soviet Union, Great Britain, and China—as well as other smaller countries joining in. America sent aid to China, thus bolstering them against the Japanese invaders. Japan then turned to Taiwan for its manpower to continue fighting. Thus, the Second Sino-Japanese War merged into World War II.

World War II and Taiwan

Japan poured a lot of work into Taiwanese industries to manufacture materials for warfare. Japan recruited Taiwanese into their military forces and later conscripted them. There was a well-known unit composed entirely of aboriginal tribes called the Takasago Volunteers who fought in World War II. The aborigines were much more accustomed to the subtropical climate of Southeast Asia and were a tremendous asset to the Japanese war effort. The Takasago Volunteers fought in the Philippines, the Dutch East Indies, the Solomon Islands, and New Guinea along with other Taiwanese and Japanese soldiers. Some of them were even part of the Kaoru Special Attack Force, a force that was specifically designated to go out on suicide missions.

The Japanese Navy operated out of Japan, and the largest unit, called the South Strike Force, was based at current-day Taiwan University.

The Battle of Midway

In early June 1942, the Americans retaliated against the Japanese Navy for its attack on Pearl Harbor by breaking the cryptic code the Japanese used. Therefore, they were able to defend themselves against the air strikes from the South Strike Force upon their aircraft carriers. This happened in the northcentral Pacific under the leadership of American General Chester Nimitz. Many Japanese personnel were lost, and four fleet carriers were torpedoed. This severely weakened the Japanese Navy.

The Cairo Declaration

In 1943, three Allied leaders—United States President Franklin Delano Roosevelt, British Prime Minister Winston Churchill, and Generalissimo Chiang Kai-shek of the Republic of China—met at Cairo to announce their objectives in World War II. Some of the goals they presented included Japanese withdrawal from Manchuria, the Penghu Islands, and Taiwan itself. Those territories the Allies wanted returned back to the Republic of China. In addition, the Allies wanted Korea to become an independent country. Korea had been annexed in the First Sino-Chinese War. The declaration stated: "With these objects in view, the three allies, in harmony with the United Nations at war with Japan, will continue to persevere in the serious and prolonged operations necessary to procure the unconditional surrender of Japan."

The Formosa Air Battle

In 1944, the United States Fast Carrier Task Force and the naval and land-based forces of Japan battled each other in the vicinity of the base for the Japanese Navy in south Taiwan. The American fighter planes bombed during the day while the Japanese bombed at night. The South Strike Force at the Japanese naval base took on the American air fighters over Taiwan.

This battle, fought between October 12th and October 16th, utilized the Third Fleet of the U.S. Navy under Admiral William Halsey Jr. and four fleets of the Imperial Japanese Navy under Vice Admirals Ryūnosuke Kusaka and Shigeru Fukudome. The Japanese used the Philippines and the city of Takao, Taiwan, as their bases. The U.S. utilized aircraft carriers along with accompanying destroyers. This battle was primarily fought in the air and on the sea, and it included bombing runs on the island of Okinawa, southwest of Taiwan, as well as a major operation on the Ryukyu Islands near Japan.

On the first day, all four divisions of the U.S. task force engaged the anti-aircraft fire over numerous runs of Japanese fighter jets around dawn. The American aircraft carriers shot down about 100 Japanese fighter planes. The Japanese pilots weren't fully trained, and that put them at an extreme disadvantage. The battle continued throughout the day and into the night when an experienced Japanese fighter squadron staged a nighttime radar-assisted air group utilizing aerial torpedoes and shot down three U.S. fighter jets; eight more Japanese jets were also destroyed. The following day was overcast, but there were nighttime air attacks.

On October 14th, there were heavy engagements during the day. Twenty-five Japanese jets flew low and came tearing out of the cloud cover without much warning. Very few Japanese aircraft survived this first wave of attacks. In the late afternoon, the American task force was again hit heavily by Japanese bombers. Two torpedoes from a Japanese plane then headed for the USS *Houston*. One of the two hit its target, and the engine room flooded. There was so much damage that some of the men dove into the water that had been roughened by the vibrations of bomb blasts and exploding shells. The *Houston* sailors were picked up by the battleship, USS *Boston*, and it was towed to Ulithi. Other American carrier groups sustained minimal damage. Not many of the other Japanese fighter planes and bombers were able to evade the American fighter aircraft.

The Japanese decided to change their strategy and started fighting from dawn to dusk against American Task Force 38. On October 15th, nearly two dozen Japanese fighter planes were shot down. The largest Japanese fighter plane attack consisted of 75 planes, but the American aircraft gun batteries kept firing incessantly.

At the end of the battle, Vice Admiral Fukudome sadly commented, "Our fighters were nothing but so many eggs thrown at the stone wall of the indomitable enemy formation." Despite his remark, the Japanese promulgated the message that they were victorious.

Further Military Campaigns in the Pacific Theater

Between 1944 and 1945, battles in the southern Pacific continued with campaigns between America and its allies against Japan. In the

Pacific, battles were fought in Japan, the Dutch East Indies, the Solomon Islands, New Guinea, the Philippines, Timor, and Borneo. Sixty-seven Japanese cities were destroyed, mostly by B-24 Liberator bombers. The B-24s were loaded with huge bombs which the soldiers rolled out through chutes. The men had to grasp handles on the side of the metal aircraft while they shoved the huge bombs out. The planes were very cold inside due to the high altitude, depending upon the season. There was one soldier who handled the upper turret with his huge gun, but he was virtually a sitting target for Japanese aircraft that defended the airspace. On the ground, U.S. war veterans, who formed the Japanese Occupation Force, indicated that there was virtually little left standing in those cities and that refugees were everywhere. They just couldn't understand why Japan wouldn't surrender.

Potsdam Declaration

In late July 1945, representatives from the United States, the Republic of China, and Great Britain proposed an agreement that would end World War II. Together, both sides lost about 36 million men in the Pacific theater and were anxious to end this war, which had been fought on two fronts, Europe and the South Pacific. The fighting in Europe had stopped in May 1945, so the only area left to be subdued was the South Pacific. The treaty proposal delineated the island of Japan and some of its nearby islands as the sovereign property of Japan, and it also stated that Japan was to withdraw its military forces from the other countries it had been occupying. Mutual withdrawal of foreign troops and equipment would be agreed upon by the Allies. The end of this declaration carried the threat of "prompt and utter destruction" to be visited upon Japan unless it was signed. This announcement was called the Potsdam Declaration, and Emperor Hirohito of Japan postponed signing it until the Soviet Union agreed to mediate it. According to one of the Japanese officials, the Japanese were responding to the proposal by remaining silent, which the Americans took to mean that they were just going to ignore it. Hence, they carried out their threat of "utter destruction."

Atomic Bombing of Hiroshima and Nagasaki

In 1938, nuclear fission was discovered, and through the efforts exerted during the Manhattan Project, a nuclear bomb was created which was capable of devastating the land for miles around the drop site. As a result of the Quebec Agreement, signed by the United Kingdom and the United States, the two countries' scientists worked together to build the nuclear bomb. By mid-July 1945, the bomb was created. On August 6th and on August 9th, the bombs were dropped on the cities of Hiroshima and Nagasaki, respectively. Most of those killed were civilians, and the total number of deaths has been estimated to be around 129,000 to 226,000 people. For months and even years afterward, the effects of nuclear radiation continued to kill people. The Japanese surrendered on August 15th, 1945.

Treaty of San Francisco

The Japanese Instrument of Surrender officially ended the hostilities of World War II. It was signed by the Empire of Japan, the United States, the Republic of China, the United Kingdom, the Soviet Union, Australia, Canada, France, the Netherlands, and New Zealand on September 2nd, 1945. The Allies still occupied Japan, marking the only time in Japan's history where it has been occupied by a foreign power. Emperor Hirohito still retained his position, though.

In September 1951, Japan and 49 Allied nations signed the Treaty of San Francisco. By virtue of this agreement, Japan was granted sovereignty over its own country and ended the Allied occupation of Japan. Japan was to allocate some money to Allied prisoners who had endured war crimes. The treaty also called for the release of prisoners of war on both sides. Japan was required to give up its assets in Taiwan, Korea, northern China, including Manchuria and other parts of northeast China, and portions of central China, including Shanghai. In addition, Japan was to compensate other countries in the South Pacific to which it did damage. America created a trusteeship for the use of the Ryuku Islands, which includes the island of Okinawa.

The political status of Taiwan was to be a renounced sovereignty according to this treaty, leaving their status as a country ambiguous.

Chapter 7 – Taiwan After World War II

John Foster Dulles, the United States secretary of state of the U.S. under President Eisenhower from 1953 to 1959, was in favor of total sovereignty for Taiwan, but allowances for that in the treaty weren't specified. Instead, it ceded the sovereignty of Taiwan to no one. Following the San Francisco Treaty, another treaty called the Treaty of Taipei was developed in April 1952. Since the Republic of China did not sign the Treaty of San Francisco, Japan was encouraged by the United States to make their own treaty with them. This treaty surrendered Japan's claim to Taiwan, and the treaty went into effect in August 1952.

Despite Taiwan not being given to any country specifically, the Republic of China had already formed the Taiwan Provincial Administrative Office in September 1945 to start the takeover process of the nation on behalf of the Allies. Chen Yi was established as the Chief Executive of the Taiwan Province in late August, and his rule was quite controversial. He had the air of an aristocrat and even refused to speak Japanese, even though the Taiwanese were fluent in the language, having learned it from their

Japanese overlords. It is said he himself wasn't corrupt, but Chen was lax in terms of the people who served in the government under him. Thus, corruption did creep in, and it grew until it was rampant.

Because of the widespread corruption, the economy of Taiwan went into a tailspin. Many were unemployed. And to make matters worse, Chinese nationals poured into the country and took jobs away from the Taiwanese. Con men wandered the streets and tried to mislead locals into fantastic schemes, thus exploiting their need for support.

The 2/28 Incident

In 1946, Chen Yi tightened his control on the government and followed the nationalization formula, with the government controlling certain industries like mining and transportation. He wanted to lessen the control of the central government, but it is difficult to determine whether that was due to his rivalry with Chinese nationalist leaders or out of a concern for Taiwan. It also did not help that those loyal to Japan, who relinquished Taiwan after World War II, were stirring the pot, creating problems and pointing out the flaws of the newly established government.

The tobacco industry was one of the many industries controlled by the government. On February 27th of 1947, a woman by the name of Lin was selling contraband cigarettes but was intercepted by some agents of the Taiwan Monopoly Bureau. She demanded the return of her cigarettes; instead, one of the agents hit her head with the butt of a pistol, beating her until she died. That enraged a crowd of onlookers, and an agent fired upon them, killing one.

The following day, February 28th, the Taiwanese participated in a peaceful protest, demanding justice. They complained at the Monopoly Bureau, but their appeals were ignored. They next moved to the governor-general's office, where four of the protestors were shot and killed with no warning. The crowd became unruly, and angry Taiwanese took over the administration of the town, broadcasting demands for more autonomy over the local radio station.

Civic leaders then organized into the "Committee to Settle the February 28th Incident" and presented their demands to the government. Outside of Taipei, the rebellion spread. Some Taiwanese even traveled to China, looting and stealing. Other Chinese came over to Taiwan, engaging in the same behavior. The 27 Brigade, under the leadership of Xie Xuehong, stole arms and grenades. While Chen Yi proclaimed his love for Taiwan on the radio and proposed to meet with the Committee, he secretly called in military troops from China to put down the rebellions. There were headless and mutilated bodies littered all over the streets. No one knows the exact number of people who died, but there are wide ranges of estimations, so it is most likely somewhere between 5,000 and 28,000. The Nationalist Army continued to fight and conducted wholesale executions resulting in about 3,000 more deaths.

Chen stated that he did not call for military support, telling this to the American ambassador, John Leighton Stuart. However, Stuart uncovered that Chen had indeed called for them, and he informed Chiang Kai-shek, who was at the KMT headquarters during this time. Due to this, Chen was dismissed and replaced by Wei Tao-ming. Following his dismissal, Chen took up various political positions. In early 1949, Chen thought the KMT would not regain its foothold and attempted to defect to the Chinese Communist Party, attempting to induce one of the commanders of a garrison to join him. This commander told Chang Kai-shek, who was furious and stripped Chen of his position. He was escorted to Taiwan in April 1950, where he was imprisoned and then later executed in June of that year.

Chen was right, though; the Communist forces would be too great to go against. In 1949, the People's Liberation Army, under Mao Zedong, inflicted great losses against the KMT forces. On October 1st, 1949, the People's Republic of China was established. In early December, Chiang Kai-shek fled to Taiwan to escape whatever the Communist Party had planned for him, leaving the control of China in the hands of Mao (although Chiang would try to gain control of it back later).

The White Terror

Martial law was declared in Taiwan in May 1949, and it continued to be in effect until the government relocated there; in fact, martial law wasn't repealed until 1987. During the White Terror, Chiang Kai-shek initiated a brutal crackdown on intellectuals and the elite based on the belief that they would object to rule by the KMT or that they were Communist sympathizers. Political groups supporting independence for Taiwan, namely the Formosan League for Reemancipation and the World United Formosans for Independence, were persecuted or imprisoned for allegedly having ties to the Communist Party. Speaking about the 2/28 massacre was forbidden, along with any form of criticism against Chiang Kai-shek's KMT. Chiang also forbade travel to China altogether.

During that period, the famous Bo Yang, a social critic and political writer, was imprisoned. He had courageously recommended the reform of the KMT and promoted human rights. The paranoia against Chinese communism was acute in Chiang Kai-shek's government.

The Battle of Kinmen

Also known as the Battle of Guningtou or the Battle of Kuningtou, this battle in late October 1949 was waged by Chiang Kai-shek and Mao Zedong. At that time, there were two governments—the Republic of China under Chiang Kai-shek and the People's Republic of China under Mao Zedong. Chiang had already been withdrawing its forces from mainland China to Taiwan since the establishment of the latter party.

ROC garrisons, however, still remained on the islands of Kinmen and Matsu, and the People's Republic believed they had to be dealt with. On these two islands in the Taiwan Strait, the two armies fought a short but bloody battle. The Republic of China's formidable battleship, *Chung Lung*, was anchored off Kinmen and pommeled the inadequate People's Republic junks and fishing boats. Once they ran out of ammunition and supplies, Mao's navy fled back to mainland China.

Members of the government under the rule of the Kuomintang and Chiang Kai-shek fled to Taiwan in December 1949 along with many civilians. About two million people had descended upon Taiwan throughout the year to reestablish themselves, hoping that they could return in the future to control mainland China.

In 1950, Chiang Kai-shek then resumed his position as president of the Republic of China, with the government now based in Taiwan, and drew up plans to retake the mainland. He called that effort "Project National Glory," but it wasn't successful.

The Struggle of Democratic Movements

In time, the Taiwanese and members of the KMT started to cooperate and resumed work on the economic recovery of the country. This was due in large part to Chiang Kai-shek's son, Chiang Ching-kuo, who assumed power in 1978 after his father's death in 1975 (Yen Chia-kan, as vice president, served in the role of president until the next election). Chiang Ching-kuo was a wiser and gentler ruler than his father. The first onslaught of transistor radios and textiles were steadily manufactured and sold overseas, and a middle class evolved.

There were also other political parties that grew up without governmental interference like the China Democratic Socialist Party, the Chinese Youth Party, and the Tangwai Movement (later called the Democratic Progressive Party). The Tangwai Movement comes from the term "Tangwai," meaning "outside the party." It fostered the attitude that the government of Taiwan should view Taiwan as a sovereign state that practices civil rights and democracy for all of its citizens, regardless of ethnic background. It stood against the "Japanization" of Taiwan that occurred when they were occupied by that country.

Although political parties were officially illegal, Chiang Ching-kuo usually practiced tolerance toward them, with some exceptions, like the Kaohsiung Incident (see below).

The Taiwan Relations Act

This act, signed by U.S. President Jimmy Carter, was approved by the U.S. Congress in 1979, and its purpose was maintaining peace and stability in the Western Pacific and "extensive, close and friendly relations" between the American people and the people of Taiwan. Because America had also given recognition to the People's Republic of China on the mainland, there was no official recognition of the Republic of China in Taiwan. However, to close that gap, the United States established the non-profit organization under the executive branch called the "American Institute of Taiwan." That group was to be America's unofficial channel for issues related to Taiwan as well as trade privileges and the maintaining of peace in the area.

Among the principles listed in the bill is a large section related to the security of Taiwan, indicating that the United States "will supply Taiwan with defense articles and services for its defense against an armed attack." America will also regard any attempt to undermine the economy or peace of Taiwan as a serious threat to the security of the western Pacific. Furthermore, it declares that it will not recognize the domination of the People's Republic of China over Taiwan. This act has been reaffirmed by all the American presidents since it was signed in by President Jimmy Carter, and it is cited by the U.S. Department of State as needed when applied to various agreements signed under its auspices.

The Kaohsiung Incident and Its Aftermath

Formosa Magazine and other politicians held pro-democracy demonstrations commemorating Human Rights Day on December 10th, 1979. The government sent in the police. The police didn't react immediately but later clashed with the crowds. Family members of Lin Yi-hsiung, a leader of the democratic movement, were killed or wounded by the KMT forces, including his mother and twin seven-year-old daughters who were stabbed to death. Many well-known leaders were arrested, beaten, and imprisoned.

Despite this crackdown, opposition to the KMT grew, and the Tangwai Movement advocated many reforms to the traditional KMT. In 1987, the common people were granted equal seats in the legislature, and all were eligible to apply for governmental posts, regardless of their political party. During that same year, martial law was lifted.

Political liberalization flourished, and civil rights groups blossomed, such as the Taiwan Women's Rescue Association, the Teachers' Human Rights Association, the Taiwan Environmental Protection Union, labor and farmers' groups, and many others. From these movements sprung a new party—the Democratic Progressive Party. Those members were originally affiliated with the Tangwai Movement.

The government attempted to quell these grassroots protests, due to the efforts of the Premier of the ROC, Hau Pei-tsun, but during 1990 to 1992, his efforts were generally ineffective, and he resigned in January 1993. Through the late 1990s, many of these social movements secured some decision-making powers within the government, like the Gender Equity Education Committee and a number of labor unions who freed themselves from corporate control.

Chapter 8 – Nascent Democracy

Lee Teng-hui succeeded Chiang Ching-kuo as president. He continued the democratization project to some extent. He emphasized Taiwanese cultural identity as being separate from China and promoted efforts to create exclusively Taiwan-based foreign relations. Lee had originally been a member of the KMT but was expelled for his pro-independence stance. He then formed the Taiwan Solidarity Union (TSU). Lee was, furthermore, totally in favor of full democracy for Taiwan and supported free elections rather than heredity as the process for selecting the country's leaders.

However, his administration and the legislature were extremely slow in initiating reforms, so it appears that Lee was only paying lip service to the cries for more liberalization. Some also believe that since Lee enjoyed good relations with Japan, being of Japanese descendancy himself, he was slow to initiate such reforms because he would rather have Japan rule over Taiwan instead.

Taiwanization

Taiwanization was a national movement to isolate the identity of Taiwan as being distinctly different from that of mainland China. It was a movement to glorify the Taiwanese culture, history, and economy. Taiwan, from the very beginning, was different. The aboriginal tribes there weren't Chinese, and the migrations from various sectors of China and Manchuria and ethnic groups came later in Taiwan's history.

Literature and poetry flourished during this movement and usually tended to reflect the growing pains of achieving a Taiwanese identity. In Lee Min-yung's poem, "If You Would Ask," he said, "If you ask what is the past of the island of Taiwan/ I will tell you/ Blood and tears drop on the history of the island of Taiwan/ If you ask" and "If you ask what is the future of the island of Taiwan/ I will tell you/ Step on your feet, the road is open to you."

Tiananmen Square Incident & the White Lily Movement

In 1989, there were pro-democracy protests staged by students of Taiwan University who traveled to Beijing. They were peaceful in the beginning, but later on, the crowds grew to tens of thousands of members. Li Peng, the Premier of the People's Republic of China, wanted to strengthen the authority of the Communist Party and opposed reforms that might undermine that. Li saw student-led protests as a threat to the central government and his economic control of the country. Orkesh Dolet, also known as Wu'erkaixi, the leader of the protest, went on national TV stating that Li Peng was ignoring the people's needs. Li Peng was furious and declared martial law and then sent in tanks and troops.

Li Peng was embarrassed by the demonstrations and had his troops crack down heavily upon the protestors. Troops fired indiscriminately upon the crowds, and a massacre ensued at Tiananmen Square. Hundreds, perhaps thousands, of people were slaughtered, and many were imprisoned.

On June 5th, 1990, one courageous young man stood in front of a huge tank moving into the square. The tank stopped, and the man then climbed on the tank and spoke with its driver, after which it tried to veer out of the column. He was eventually removed by the police, and his fate is unknown. The British press later identified him as Wang Weilin, a 19-year-old student, but the newspaper noted that they weren't actually sure of his identity. He remains today a hero of democracy in China.

The event is memorialized annually in Taiwan, and Tsai Ing-wen, the current president of Taiwan, said in 1989, "Freedom-loving people in Hong Kong and China rest assured that, despite threats and subversion, Taiwan will unconditionally defend democracy and safeguard freedom."

Economic Cooperation Framework Agreement (ECFA)

This agreement, signed in 2010 by Taiwan and China, was an attempt to normalize economic relations between the Republic of China and the People's Republic of China and create guidelines for trade between the two entities. This deal was seen as an impressive agreement because the two sides did not recognize each other as "countries" after the Chinese Civil War ended in 1949.

When negotiators discussed the goals of the ECFA, it did result in some protests and even fistfights in the conference room, as there were some parties in Taiwan who feared that China would use it as a means to control Taiwan.

The economic cooperation portion of the ECFA includes investment, investment cooperation, customs procedures, and food safety, among other things. Tariff reductions were featured as a means by which both countries would develop. As many as 235 products were made exempt from tariffs, and others were granted tariff reductions.

Some services, such as accounting, airplane maintenance, computer-related services, and various maintenance and repair services, were given a number of mutual benefits subsidized by the governments. Chinese-Taiwanese partnerships were encouraged.

Banks and financial institutions were openly set up in the two countries. That included subsidiaries in each country which facilitated business in the other.

Technological and R&D agencies and companies are not only protected from interference but promoted as a valuable asset to conduct business around the world. Intellectual property rights are spelled out in this agreement, although there is more protection for Taiwanese intellectual rights than Chinese. Rules and regulations were established along with a mechanism for enforcement. Today, there is much editorializing and discussion about making the ECFA more open to some foreign countries, including the United States.

The Democratic Progressive Party

Founded in the year 1986, the Democratic Progressive Party (DPP) stood for Taiwanese independence, and it also advocated social welfare policies, education, and frameworks for increasing the financial advantage of the people. The DPP firmly rejects the "One China" policy, a policy which states that there is only one state under the name of China.

In the 2000 presidential election in Taiwan, a member of the DPP, Chen Shui-bian, became president. During his administration, he pledged what was called the "Four Noes and One Without Policy," which meant that—provided that the PRC doesn't go to war with Taiwan—1) he would not institute Taiwanese independence, 2) would not change the name of the country from the Republic of China to the Republic of Taiwan, 3) not include the doctrine of special states to state relations, and 4) would not promote an effort toward reunification or independence. Chen served two terms, but scandals rocked his second term, which helped to cause his party to lose in the next election.

In the 2008 election, Ma Ying-jeou was voted in as the new president. He was from the conservative KMT but wanted to warm cross-straits relations for economic reasons. Although he does favor reunification of China and Taiwan, he has reservations about it because of the Tiananmen Square incident. As for independence, he claimed that the final decision must be made by the Taiwanese people. Ma was re-elected for another term.

The 1992 Consensus

In 1992, the head of the security council under Ma Ying-jeou attempted to define the nature of the relationship and cooperation between mainland China and Taiwan. In this consensus, the Republic of China issued its own view on the "One China" policy. They agreed that there is only one China, but each side has its own views on which is the "one China." The People's Republic of China, who is in control of mainland China, argues that they are the "one China" and refuses to acknowledge the Republic of China in Taiwan. However, both sides agree that Taiwan belongs to China, although, as can be seen, no side can agree on which one is actually the "one China."

Members of the DPP took issue with the decision of the consensus. Since there was no agreement on which government represents the "one China," then there truly was no consensus at all. In the November 2018 issue of *The Diplomat*, a Taiwanese journal, states, "Unfortunately, there is no Taiwanese consensus on the definition of the 1992 Consensus." Hence, the readers of history and current Asian events are left in a pure fog. However, in their survey, *The Diplomat* indicated that 75% of the people of Taiwan want Taiwan and China to be perceived as two different countries.

In 2016, Taiwan elected its first female president, Tsai Ing-wen. She is a member of the Democratic Progressive Party and still is serving today. Tsai has ancestors who were aborigines from the Paiwan tribe.

Taiwan Today

President Tsai has rejected the 1992 Consensus. She perceives the People's Republic of China as being a communist country interested in "putting the squeeze" on Taiwan. The PRC has cut off their relationship since Tsai took office in 2016, and it has banned

Chinese individuals from going to Taiwan. Beijing has also sent warships to the general area and conducted international relations in such a way as to cut off ties between Taiwan and other countries. Within the last ten years, China has repeatedly threatened the "use of force" if Taiwan declares independence. The U.S. Seventh Fleet also patrols the area.

As of this writing, Taiwan has signed an agreement with United States President Donald Trump to purchase weapons from the U.S. through the provisions of the Taiwan Relations Act, which clearly states that the United States may sell them to Taiwan for defensive purposes.

The People's Republic of China vs. the Republic of China (Taiwan)

In the June 2019 U.S. Department of Defense Report, it was noted that the People's Republic of China has been placing obstacles in front of Taiwan in terms of participation in international forums and health organization councils. Jonathan Moore of the U.S. Department of State has said, "Excluding 23 million Taiwanese people from these efforts runs counter to the very ethos of the international organizations we support." Little by little, the People's Republic has been quietly trying to shut off channels of communication between itself and Taiwan. America has stayed relatively mute on the subject due to the fact that the U.S. is attempting to create some amended trade agreements, in addition to new ones, with China.

Conclusion

Since 3000 BCE, the island of Taiwan has endured enormous changes. Its economy, society, and government have changed faster than it can adjust. Hence, it is a "country" that is neither a "country" nor a "state" by strict international definition. Although the Taiwanese call this condition the "status quo," it isn't a "status quo" at all. Politically, Taiwan straddles the fence between democracy and autocracy. It exists in the fog of ambiguity.

Taiwan's political status today is so ambiguous due to all the pulls and pushes from the various outside and inside forces that manage this almost 14,000-square-mile island. Taiwan is officially called the Republic of China, but it is inhabited by many varied ethnic groups. Although it carries the term "China," it is separate from mainland China. It is a country torn between the political preferences for the unification of mainland China and Taiwan and for Taiwanese independence. The KMT is still operating, and the Democratic Progressive Party (DPP) is the second-largest party. The DPP has as its primary goal the total independence of Taiwan, while the KMT has as its goal the reunification of China and Taiwan. However, due to intense pressure from the international community, specifically the United States, Japan, and the EU, it hasn't been able to recognize Taiwan as an independent country or nation-state.

However, looking past the issue of their political state, one can see that the Taiwanese are hard-working, ambitious, and intelligent people. Taiwan is a haven for artists, poets, and political scientists. It encourages developments in technologically-advanced fields and maintains a fierce and loyal spirit. It is an island that is awash in a melding of many Asiatic ethnic groups all the way from Manchuria to the islands in the South Pacific. The tension of its political stance is extreme, though, because of its modest size and location. In 2018, the journal *China Power* referred to Taiwan as an "evolving democracy," an apt term for a country that most likely still has evolving to do.

Here are two other books by Captivating History that we think you would find interesting

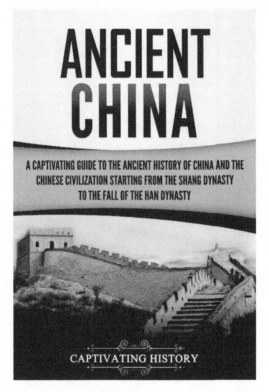

SUMERIANS

A CAPTIVATING GUIDE TO ANCIENT SUMERIAN HISTORY, SUMERIAN MYTHOLOGY AND THE MESOPOTAMIAN EMPIRE OF THE SUMER CIVILIZATION

CAPTIVATING HISTORY

Bibliography

"Losing your Head among the Tattooed Headhunters of Taiwan," Retrieved from https://www.larskrutak.com/loosing-your-head-among-the-tattooed-headhunters-of-taiwan/

Blust, R. (1999) "Subgrouping, Circularity and Extinction: Some Issues in Austronesian Comparative Linguistics: In E. Zeithoun, P. K. Ki (eds), *Selected Papers from the Eighth International Conference on Austronesian Linguistics, Taipei.* Academia Sinca, pp. 31-94

Chiu, Hsin-hui (2008) *The Colonial Civilizing Process in Dutch Formosa, 1624-1662* Brill.

Jiao, T. (2007) *The Neolithic of Southeast China: Cultural Transformation and Regional Interaction on the Coast.* Cambria Press

Katz, P. (2005) *When the Valleys Turned Blood Red: The Tapani Incident in Colonial Taiwan.* University of Hawaii Press

Singh, G. (2010) "Kuomintang, Democratization and the One-China Principle," in Sharma, A. Chakrabarti, S. (eds) *Taiwan Today,* Anthem Press

Hsu, Wen-hsiung (1980) "From Aboriginal Island to Chinese Frontier: The Development of Taiwan before 1683," In Knapp, R. (ed) *China's Island Frontier: Studies in the Historical Geography of Taiwan.* University Press of Hawaii.

Takekoshi, Y. (1907) *Japanese Rule in Formosa.* Green and Company.

Wong, E. & Edmonson, C. (2019) "Trump Administration Plans to Sell More Than $2 Billion of Arms to Taiwan," In *New York Times*, June 2, 2019. Retrieved from https://www.nytimes.com/2019/06/06/us/politics/trump-taiwan-arms-sale.html

"What does 1992 Consensus Mean to Citizens?" Retrieved from https://thediplomat.com/2018/11/what-does-the-1992-consensus-mean-to-citizens-in-taiwan/

"South China Sea: China Breaks from a Century of Humiliation," Retrieved from https://oxfordre.com/asianhistory/view/10.1093/acrefore/9780190277727.001.0001/acrefore-9780190277727-e-157

Moore, J. (2019) "Taiwan at 'Cross-Strait Relations: Present Challenges and Future Developments." *U. S. Department of Defense Report, July 2, 2019*

McGovern, J. M. (1898) *Among the Headhunters of Formosa* Prabhat Prakashan.

"President Tsai Ing-wen Promises to Defend Democracy as Taiwan Marks 30th Anniversary of the Tiananmen Crackdown," In *South China Morning Post, June 4, 2019*. Retrieved from https://www.scmp.com/news/china/diplomacy/article/3013105/president-tsai-ing-wen-promises-defend-democracy-taiwan-marks